D0549011

# Being Frog

by April Pulley Sayre

Beach Lane Books • New York  London  Toronto  Sydney  New Delhi

BEACH LANE BOOKS

An imprint of Simon & Schuster Children's Publishing Division
1230 Avenue of the Americas, New York, New York 10020
Copyright © 2020 by April Pulley Sayre
BEACH LANE BOOKS is a trademark of Simon & Schuster, Inc.
For information about special discounts for bulk purchases, please contact Simon & Schuster Special Sales
at 1-866-506-1949 or business@simonandschuster.com.
The Simon & Schuster Speakers Bureau can bring authors to your live event.
For more information or to book an event, contact the Simon & Schuster Speakers Bureau
at 1-866-248-3049 or visit our website at www.simonspeakers.com.
Book design by Lauren Rille
The text for this book was set in Didot LT Std.
Manufactured in China
1119 SCP
First Edition
10 9 8 7 6 5 4 3 2 1
Library of Congress Cataloging-in-Publication Data
Names: Sayre, April Pulley, author.
Title: Being frog / April Pulley Sayre.
Description: First edition. | New York : Beach Lane Books, [2020] | Audience: Age 3–8. | Audience: K to Grade 3. | Includes
bibliographical references and index.
Identifiers: LCCN 2019010139 | ISBN 9781534428812 (hardcover : alk. paper) | ISBN 9781534428829 (eBook)
Subjects: LCSH: Frogs—Juvenile literature. | Frogs—Life cycles—Juvenile literature.
Classification: LCC QL668.E2 S265 2020 | DDC 597.8/9—dc23 LC record available at https://lccn.loc.gov/2019010139

For Jeff

A frog

is a being.

It is watching.

It is seeing.

A frog has favorites.

This rock.

This log.

Its daily job?

Support the frog.

A frog must hunt.

It scans. It spies.

It crawls. It lunges.

It fails. Retries.

It cools in shade

beneath a flower.

It hides underwater.

Bath or shower?

It kicks and surfaces.

Its eyeballs gaze.

Does it remember

tadpole days?

First egg,

then tadpole.

Two legs. Four.

A tiny froglet

climbed ashore.

Now it suns.

It cave-spelunks.

A green frog calls

with

**glunk**

**glunk**

**glunks.**

It climbs a cliff.

Mossy. Steep.


It sits so still.

Then, suddenly—

LEAP!

Does it ponder?

We don't yet know.

Does frog time fly?

Or trail, snail-slow?

Waiting. Watching.

Scanning. Seeing.

A frog has a life.

A frog is a being.

# AUTHOR'S NOTE

In many children's books, a frog is a character. It has human thoughts and habits. It is basically a human in a frog suit. I love these imaginary frogs, but I also like real ones. Real frogs are not humans. But they are not toys, either. They are animals. They are alive. They are beings.

Every week I watch and photograph the frogs in a local pond. My husband and I have observed them for so long that we now recognize certain frogs' faces and body patterns. We call the big male with the yellow throat Lemon. (Male green frogs have a yellow throat and female green frogs have a white throat.) We call the smaller female that hunts from the cave beneath the rocks Pickle. The larger brown female that hunts atop the rocks is Bronze. Certain frogs choose to hunt from particular logs or rocks and defend these favored spots. If we cannot see the throat of the frog, we can tell whether it's male or female by its ear discs. The ear discs of males are a lot larger than their eyes. Females' ear discs are only a little bigger than their eyes.

The kinds of things we learn from observing these frogs are anecdotal evidence, meaning they are individual events. They are single observations and stories, not the careful data a scientist gathers when she or he creates a study. In order to be objective, science often skims over animals as individuals. A scientist who goes out and looks at, tags, or tests frogs rarely gets to know a frog as an individual. The scientist is looking for things about frogs that apply to all frogs.

## Life with Frogs

The local frogs see us so often that they barely move as I approach to photograph them. But, frankly, this species of frog, the green frog (*Rana clamitans*) tends to be mellow. It's a sit-and-wait predator. So it sits a lot! Some other kinds of frogs are more likely to hop. (Frogs don't always hop. They often crawl, too.)

These frogs also seem to respond to us at times. Once when I sneezed, Lemon, who had his back to me, did a sudden 180-degree turn to face me, then took three hops toward me and made a loud *glunk!*

Notice that I say "seem" to respond. That is because two events (my sneeze and Lemon's call) can happen near the same time, but not be related. This is called a coincidence. I cannot prove a link without further study.

I only know from observation that Lemon sometimes

reacts, seemingly in protest, if we are loud. Again, I say "seemingly in protest." I do not know his motivation, his innermost frog thoughts. I do not know if he is really annoyed with us for interfering with his hunting success. After all, what if there was a female frog Lemon was courting behind me in the grass, and Lemon was hopping in her direction instead? True scientific study would find out if there are links between these events, or if they were just a writer's imaginings while sitting watching frogs far too long.

Yet wondering and imagining are a part of science too. They help a scientist come up with creative questions. Could an adult frog remember tadpole days? The idea sounds far-fetched. But science is full of surprises. Dr. Martha Weiss trained hornworm caterpillars to avoid a stinky gas. Afterward, the caterpillars entered cocoons and became moths. The adult, winged moths avoided the stinky gas too. So, if an adult moth can remember something from being a caterpillar, perhaps an adult frog could remember something from being a tadpole! A scientist would go beyond pondering and design an experiment to find the truth.

For now, we will keep spending time with the frogs. After getting to know all these frogs "in person," so to speak, I still like imaginary frog characters in books and movies. But for me a made-up frog cannot match the beauty of a real frog—a creature so alive in its pond world.

## Resources for Further Exploration

Learning to identify frogs' calls can help you locate them. Renowned sound recordist Lang Elliott has created books and CDs teaching frog and toad calls as well as an app called Pure Nature - 3D Soundscapes, which can be found at musicofnature.com.

Search for books about amphibians in your state or region. Regional guides to vernal ponds, the temporary ponds that form from spring rains, also cover frogs and sometimes tadpole identification.

To learn more about worldwide frog conservation, visit:

Amphibian Ark: amphibianark.org

Amphibian Survival Alliance: amphibians.org

EDGE of Existence: edgeofexistence.org/species

National Geographic Kids: nationalgeographic.com/animals amphibians